INDIAN SCHOOL
TEACHING THE WHITE MAN'S WAY

MICHAEL L. COOPER

CLARION BOOKS

New York

to a marvelous friend,
BILHA GOODMAN

Clarion Books
a Houghton Mifflin Company imprint
215 Park Avenue South, New York, NY 10003
Copyright © 1999 by Michael L. Cooper

The text has been set in 12-point Fairfield Light.

Book design by Richard Granald.

For information about permission
to reproduce selections from this book,
write to Permissions, Houghton Mifflin Company,
215 Park Avenue South, New York, NY 10003.

Printed in the USA.

Library of Congress Cataloging-in-Publication Data

Cooper, Michael L., 1950–
    Indian school : teaching the white man's way / by Michael L.
Cooper
    p.   cm.
    Includes bibliographical references.
    ISBN 0-395-92084-1
  1. Indians of North America—Education—Juvenile literature.
2. Off-reservation boarding schools—United States—Juvenile literature.
3. Indians of North America—Cultural assimilation—Juvenile literature.
I. Title
E97.5.C66 1999   98-43640
370'.8997—dc21   CIP

EB 10 9 8 7 6 5 4 3 2 1

CONTENTS

ACKNOWLEDGMENTS

Special thanks to Vyrtis Thomas at the Smithsonian Institution; Linda Witmar, Richard L. Tritt, and Barbara C. Landis at the Cumberland County Historical Society in Carlisle, Pennsylvania; William A. Mehojah Jr., Deputy Director, Office of Indian Education, Department of the Interior; Donzella Maupin and Cynthia Poston at the Hampton University Archives; Sally Foster for her photographic services; Marilyn Courtot for her bibliographical research; and Mike Duniven for his expert editorial comments.

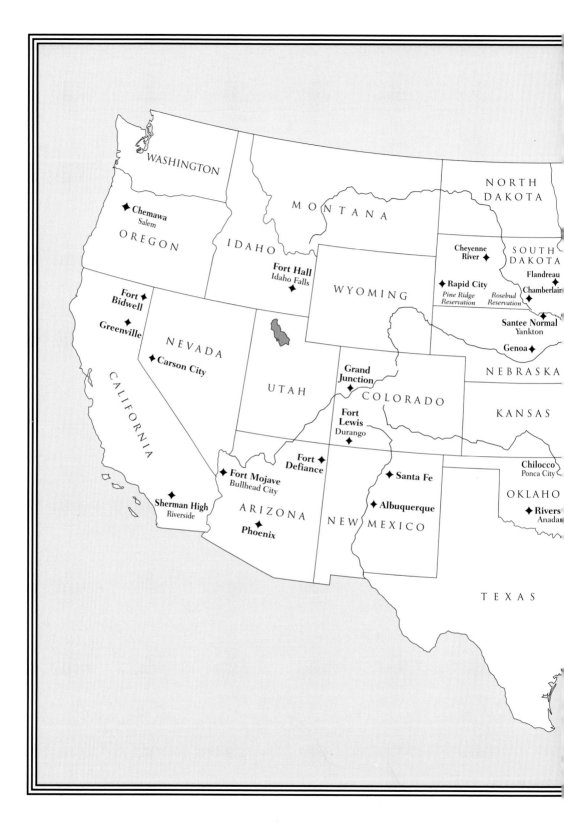

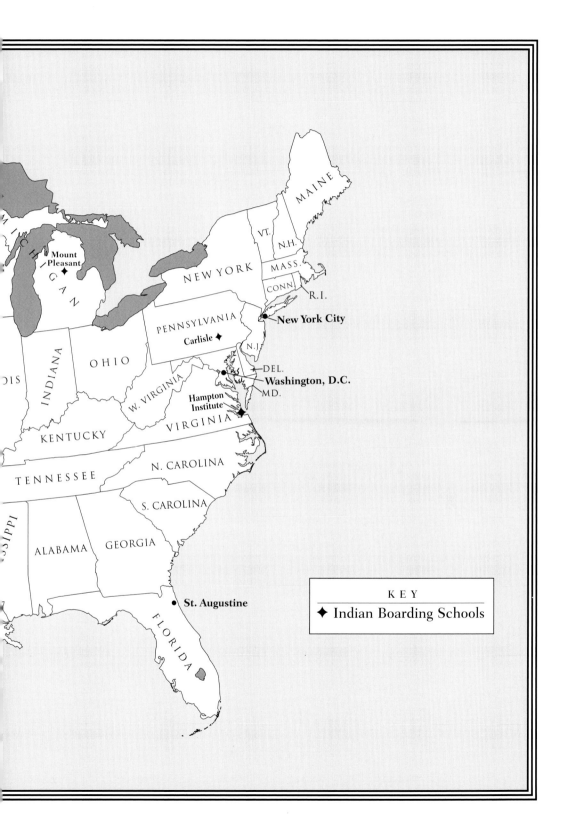

MAINE

VT.

N.H.

MASS.

CONN

R.I.

NEW YORK

Mount
Pleasant ◆

MICHIGAN

PENNSYLVANIA

Carlisle ◆

● New York City

N.J.

OHIO

INDIANA

DIS

W. VIRGINIA

DEL.

● Washington, D.C.

MD.

Hampton
Institute ◆

KENTUCKY

VIRGINIA

TENNESSEE

N. CAROLINA

S. CAROLINA

SSIPPI

ALABAMA

GEORGIA

● St. Augustine

FLORIDA

KEY

◆ Indian Boarding Schools

1

ON THE WHITE MAN'S ROAD

"I COULD THINK OF NO REASON why white people wanted Indian boys and girls except to kill them, and not having the remotest idea of what a school was, I thought we were going east to die."

These were the thoughts of an eleven-year-old boy named Ota Kte as he and eighty-three other young Sioux journeyed the thousand miles from their homes on the Great Plains to a boarding school in the small town of Carlisle, Pennsylvania.

Ota Kte, a Lakota Sioux, had good reason to be afraid. The year was 1879. For most of the boy's life, the seven tribes of the Teton Sioux had been fighting white people. Only three years earlier, in one of their biggest battles, Sioux and Cheyenne warriors had killed Lieutenant Colonel George Armstrong Custer and 250 soldiers near the Little Bighorn River in the Montana Territory. There was more fighting after the Battle of the Little Bighorn, but the Indians could not defeat the U.S. Army, which was much larger than the Indian forces. "I thought if we killed all of the white men we saw that no more would come," one chief said. "We killed all we could, but they came more and more, like new grass in the spring."

The army was trying to protect the growing number of whites moving into Sioux territory. This vast area included what are now North and South Dakota and parts of present-day Montana, Wyoming, Nebraska, and Minnesota. The army forced the Sioux chiefs to sign a treaty under which they agreed to give up most of their land. In return, the treaty gave the tribes a reservation nearly the size of South Dakota. This large reservation included the sacred Black Hills. Indians believed that these rugged, forest-covered mountains were the holiest spot on earth. Only a couple of years later, however, prospectors discovered gold there, and the government took the Black Hills away from the Sioux. The chiefs were still angry about losing the sacred land when a soldier came to ask for their children.

Captain Richard Henry Pratt arrived at Rosebud Reservation in late September 1879, a time when cold autumn winds were beginning to sweep across the northern plains. In previous years, the Sioux would have been preparing for the long winter ahead. The men would have killed hundreds of buffalo and the women would have been busy drying the meat and tanning the hides. But those old ways were gone. Now tribal leaders faced a new challenge—the future of their children.

Forty warriors and chiefs met with Captain Pratt in the council house at the reservation. Among them were White Thunder,

Two Strike, and the most respected and powerful Brulé chief, Spotted Tail. These men knew Pratt was a warrior too. He had led the famous Buffalo Soldiers, a cavalry troop of black soldiers and Indian scouts who fought Comanches and Apaches in Texas and in the neighboring Territory of New Mexico.

Captain Pratt spoke through an interpreter to the assembled warriors. He proposed taking their sons and daughters back east, where they would learn English and be taught how to live like white people.

The chiefs listened patiently as the interpreter explained Pratt's words. Afterward, Spotted Tail rose. He was a stocky, brown-skinned man about fifty-five years old. In Sioux, the chief spoke sternly to the army officer. "The white people are all thieves and liars. We do not want our children to learn such things. The white man is very smart. He knew there was gold in the Black Hills and he made us agree to give up all that country, and now a great many white people are there getting out the gold."

Captain Pratt listened quietly to the harsh criticism. When Spotted Tail finished talking, the captain, a tall, lean fellow about fifteen years younger than the Brulé leader, faced the chief and replied, "Spotted Tail, you are a remarkable man. You are such an able man that you are the principal chief of these thousands of your people. But, Spotted Tail, you cannot read or write. You cannot speak the language of this country. . . . Because you were not educated, these mountains, valleys, and streams have passed from you. Your ignorance against the white man's education will more and more hinder and restrain you and take from you."

The captain finished speaking and left the lodge so the chiefs could discuss his proposition. Some argued that their children would forget how to be Indians if they went away to the school. Others said that it was necessary to learn the white man's ways in order for their people to survive. After an hour, they finally agreed to send their sons and daughters to the faraway school.

Hundreds of Sioux gathered a few days later at Rosebud Landing on the Missouri River to say goodbye to the young people traveling east with Captain Pratt. Many of them were the children and grandchildren of well-known chiefs such as White Thunder and the great Oglala warrior Red Cloud. Pratt's army commanders had told him to take as many of the chiefs' children as possible because it would make the tribes easier to control. The Sioux had been on the warpath only three years earlier, and there was a chance they might make war again.

It was customary for the Sioux to celebrate significant events with presents. The children's parents gave cloth and food to their fellow tribespeople. Spotted Tail, who was sending four children and two grandchildren to Carlisle, gave away a beautiful young horse.

After tearful goodbyes with mothers and fathers, the eighty-four boys and girls of all ages boarded a steamboat, which carried them down the Missouri River to Yankton, on the southeastern

This drawing depicts how one boy, who had been participating in a tribal ceremony, looked when Captain Pratt first talked to him about attending boarding school. ARMY WAR COLLEGE

edge of what is now South Dakota. There the group boarded a train traveling eastward toward the sprawling cities crowded with white people.

So much along the way was new for the young Indians. None of them had ever been on a train, which they called an iron horse. They rode in two private cars to avoid the curious stares of other passengers, but it was a scary trip nonetheless. "We held our blankets between our teeth," Ota Kte explained, "because our hands were both busy hanging on to the seats, so frightened were we."

The first time the young people left the train to eat dinner, they attracted a lot of attention. The older boys had painted their faces and put feathers in their hair. They all wore their regular clothing: beads, blankets, and buffalo-hide leggings and moccasins. A crowd of whites, excited about seeing the children of such famous chiefs as Spotted Tail and Red Cloud, followed them down the street.

"I suppose," Ota Kte said, "many of these people expected to see us coming with scalping knives between our teeth, bows and arrows in one hand and tomahawk in the other, and to hear a great war cry as we came off that iron horse."

A police escort protected the Indians from the curious crowd. "Back of the rows of uniformed men," Ota Kte said, "stood the white people craning their necks, talking, laughing, and making a great noise." It was frightening to be surrounded by so many strange people. The children pulled their blankets tightly around their shoulders and walked close together for safety.

Even after the youngsters were inside the restaurant, people gathered outside on the sidewalk to stare through the window. Captain Pratt's group puzzled over the long tables covered with white cloths and set with plates, cups, knives, and forks. They were not accustomed to eating this way. Nor did they like being watched by the rude crowd. The older boys wrapped the food in their blankets and led the whole group back to the train to eat.

Near the end of the four-day journey to Pennsylvania, everyone was bored and restless. The big boys, Ota Kte recalled, "began to tell us little fellows that the white people were taking us to the place where the sun rises, where they would dump us over the edge of the earth, as we had been taught that the earth was flat, with four corners, and when we came to the edge, we would fall over."

To everyone's surprise, it began to appear that this story was true. On the last evening of their trip, a full moon rose in front of the train. It loomed just above the horizon and appeared to be exceptionally large. Were they really near the earth's edge? They began singing a tribal song to bolster their courage. Despite their fear, the smaller children were so exhausted they fell asleep. The older boys soon shook them awake and pointed up at the sky. The moon was now behind them. Had they passed the spot where it rested during the day? Ota Kte later learned that the train had simply switched directions, from east to southwest, toward Carlisle.

They arrived on the evening of October 6, 1879. Hundreds of curious citizens gathered at the station to welcome the first Indians the town had seen in many decades. The young Sioux,

The first group of girls who traveled with Captain Pratt from their villages in the Dakota Territory to the Indian school in Carlisle, Pennsylvania.

The first Sioux boys, soon after arriving at Carlisle.

followed by many of the townspeople, walked the short distance to the old army barracks that would be their school.

Ota Kte was the first student to step onto the school grounds. "I was thrust into an alien world," he explained, "into an environment as different from the one into which I was born as it is possible to imagine, to remake myself if I could into the likeness of the invader."

Years later, Ota Kte and many other Native Americans wrote about their experiences as students at Carlisle and other government boarding schools. Although their accounts expressed mixed feelings about school and the white man's ways, they all shared a common regret—the loss of their Indian heritage.

2

THE INDIAN WAY

THE YOUNG NATIVE AMERICANS who left their homes to attend
boarding school were not only leaving their families, they were
also leaving a way of life. They would see their parents again, but
traditional Indian ways were rapidly disappearing.

Indian children developed strong ties to their people and to
their land at a very young age. Soon after a girl named Goes to War
With was born, her parents held a two-day party called a Blessing
Way. This old Navajo ceremony was intended to instill good char-
acter, especially generosity and hospitality, in the child. The girl's
mother prepared a feast and medicine men sang songs while the
girl's father gave blankets, jewelry, and other gifts to friends and
neighbors.

These guests were part of an extended family described by one
person as a "warm blanket of kin." They included grandparents,
uncles, aunts, and cousins, all of whom helped the mother and

11

A Shoshone family in their tepee. This photograph was taken in 1871 in the region now called Idaho. SMITHSONIAN INSTITUTION

father watch over Goes to War With and teach her skills she would need as an adult. Many Native Americans remembered their first lessons.

Gertrude Simmons, who was not given an Indian name because her father was a white man, recalled that at age seven she was "as free as the wind that blew my hair, and no less spirited than a bounding deer." Yet the child, whose mother was Yankton Sioux, was neither too young nor too spirited to start learning the responsibilities of the women in her tribe. "Close beside my

A Hopi child learns by working beside her mother and other women in the close-knit tribe. NATIONAL ARCHIVES

mother I sat on a rug with a scrap of buckskin in one hand and an awl in the other. This was the beginning of my practical observation lessons in the art of beadwork."

A thousand miles away, in an area that is now Arizona, lived a Hopi named Nakavoma. The men and women of his tribe farmed and raised sheep. They were also skilled artisans who wove their wool into blankets decorated with geometrical designs. By the time he was ten years old, Nakavoma had woven his first blanket, and his parents had given him a small section of the family's corn and watermelon patch to care for.

Many Indian boys wanted to grow up to be fearless hunters and warriors who would protect their people from all enemies. Warriors were men of great influence, entitled to honor and privilege. "I wished to be a brave man as much as a white boy desires to be a great lawyer or even president of the United States," said a young Santee Sioux named Ohiyesa. "Our games were feats with the bow and arrows, foot and pony races, wrestling, swimming and imitation of the customs and habits of our fathers."

Indian boys played these games for only a few years before assuming adult responsibilities. When they were teenagers, Native Americans married, had children, and went on the warpath.

Jason Betzinez was a thirteen-year-old Apache boy when Geronimo, one of the last chiefs to wage prolonged war against white men, asked him to go along on a war party. "I was now old enough to be a warrior, and the way to learn was to go on several raids with an experienced man, taking care of his horses and equipment, standing guard, and cooking his meat for him," he explained. "That was the Apache custom."

It is not surprising that Native American boys aspired to be warriors. "They were all keen, athletic young men, tall and lean and brave," reported an army officer visiting a Crow encampment, "and I admired them as real specimens of manhood more than any body of men I have ever seen before or since."

The Crows, this officer also observed, like most plains tribes, were "rich in everything an Indian required to make him happy." The source of their wealth was obvious: hundreds of thousands of buffalo that roamed the Great Plains. The Indians depended on these animals, which weighed as much as two thousand pounds,

An Indian boy before being introduced to the white man's way.
HAMPTON UNIVERSITY ARCHIVES

for food, shelter, and clothing. They used every part of the buffalo, even braiding the hair into ropes and carving the bones into knives.

By the time the first Sioux students traveled to Carlisle, the huge herds were disappearing. "Wherever the whites are established," observed one chief, "the buffalo is gone and the red hunter must die of hunger." White hunters such as "Buffalo Bill" Cody killed thousands of the animals just for their hides. The

An oil painting of a Blackfoot encampment, probably in Montana. The women in the center are preparing a buffalo skin for tanning. It is titled "The Silk Rope" and was painted by Charles M. Russell about 1890.
AMON CARTER MUSEUM, FORT WORTH

government encouraged the slaughter, hoping that with no buffalo to hunt, the Indians would stay on their reservations and stop fighting with white settlers.

The growing number of whites moving into the western territories caused big declines in the Native American population. Many Indians were killed in battles with the newcomers. Even more deadly were contagious diseases such as tuberculosis and scarlet

Sioux girls in traditional dress. SMITHSONIAN INSTITUTION

fever, which had been unknown among Indians before the arrival of whites. The number of Native Americans in North America declined from more than a million people at the beginning of the nineteenth century to fewer than three hundred thousand in 1879.

Conquered by white people, America's Indians became wards of the U.S. government. They lived on reservations under the control of the Bureau of Indian Affairs in Washington, D.C. The BIA gave them white people's cast-off clothing and monthly rations of fatback, coffee, and hardtack. BIA agents ordered Native

The coming of white people, who slaughtered the buffalo, forever changed the Indian way of life. LIBRARY OF CONGRESS

Americans to give up their old ways, even their religion. White people wanted Indians to replace their tepees with houses and their bows and arrows with plows.

"When I had reached young manhood," Ohiyesa lamented, "the warpath was a thing of the past. The hunter had disappeared with the buffalo, the war scout had lost his calling, and the warrior had taken his shield to the mountaintop and given it back to the elements. The victory songs were sung only in memory of the

Sioux children, looking less than enthusiastic, on their first day of school. LIBRARY OF CONGRESS

braves. So I could not prove I was brave and would fight to protect my home and land."

Everyone, Native Americans as well as white people, knew that the Indian way of life was disappearing. The pressing question in the late nineteenth century was what to do about the "Indian problem." One government official believed that, "we must either butcher them or civilize them." For Captain Pratt, there was only one choice.

3

CARLISLE AND THE
INDIAN SCHOOL IDEA

Captain Pratt had been a frontier Indian fighter before becoming an educator. Yet even as the founder of the Carlisle Industrial School for Indians, he was still waging a kind of war.

Rather than killing Native Americans or confining them to reservations, he now wanted them to forget their traditions and begin living like white people. The sooner all tribal relations were broken up and the sooner the Indians lost all their old ways, even their language, Captain Pratt believed, the better their lives would be.

Young Indians would forget their past, the captain thought, if they were educated far from their "savage" environment. And Carlisle was a long way from the reservations in the western territories. The Pennsylvania town was nestled in the Cumberland Valley two hundred miles southwest of America's biggest city, New York, and one hundred miles northwest of the nation's capital, Washington, D.C.

Captain Richard Pratt, who was called the father of Indian education. ARMY WAR COLLEGE

On the edge of Carlisle sat a post built by the British Army 130 years earlier. It had sheltered troops that were fighting Indians who lived in the region at the time. More recently, Confederate soldiers in the Civil War had partially burned the post. That war's bloodiest engagement, at Gettysburg, was fought a few miles to the south. After the war, the post had sat mostly unused until Captain Pratt persuaded the army to let him turn the old buildings into the federal government's first Native American boarding school.

The twenty-three-acre campus consisted of several barracks, stables, a hospital, a bakery, a dining room, a coal house, and a guardhouse. The Indian boys helped carpenters fix up two barracks for dormitories and a third for classrooms. They converted the stables to workshops, where instructors taught printing, wagon-making, shoemaking, carpentry, and a dozen other trades.

Captain Pratt was the vital force behind the boarding school. He oversaw the remodeling, traveled west to recruit more students, and visited Washington to persuade government officials to provide more money for Indian education. Although the government funded Carlisle and the other Indian schools that were soon established, the students contributed by cleaning, cooking, and doing all of the routine jobs performed by paid staffs at other boarding schools.

It was ironic that Pratt, a forty-year-old professional soldier, was running his own school, because the Indiana native did not even have a high school diploma. As a young man, Pratt had enlisted in the Union Army eight days after the Civil War began, in April 1861. After the war, he decided to make the service his career. He was assigned to lead the Tenth Cavalry, the Buffalo Soldiers, fighting Indians in the southwest.

Captain Pratt became interested in educating Native Americans in the mid-1870s, when he took seventy-two Indian prisoners to Fort Marion in St. Augustine, Florida. The imprisoned Kiowa, Apache, Cheyenne, and Comanche warriors were so unhappy there that they began to die. Pratt knew he had to make some changes in order to save their lives.

Indian prisoners, soon after their arrival in 1875 at Fort Marion, Florida. CUMBERLAND COUNTY HISTORICAL SOCIETY

January 21, 1878
St. Augustine, Fla.

General S. C. Armstrong
Principal Hampton N. and A. Institute

Dear Sir:

I write to aid Mrs. Camthers who wishes to know just what advancement will be required to admit two or more of the Indians to your school, and the smallest sum required to cover the yearly expenses, so that application may be made to the Indian office. I hope the requirements and terms are such as will enable Mrs. C — to provide for five or six, and that you can receive that many. Indeed it would be a grand thing if fifteen or twenty could go. They are young men of nineteen to twenty six years, who were regular blanket Indians when brought here from the plains, May 21, '75, and belong to Kiowa, Comanche, Cheyenne and Arapahoe tribes, who, up to the time these were arrested, had scarcely accepted any of the government's advancements of civilization. They now read and write and speak our language with some understanding and hunger after knowledge and usefulness. They are as thoroughly obedient and willing to work as any class of men and in this respect will soon be able to hold their own with your colored youth, so that favorable estimates can be made on that head. These would be no drawbacks on account of color.

We hear rumors that lead us to hope for your personal examination during the winter.

With great respect, Sincerely yours,
R. H. Pratt

Letter to the principal of Hampton Institute, praising the Indian prisoners as able students. HAMPTON UNIVERSITY ARCHIVES

The captain organized his prisoners into military-style companies and designated several of them as officers in charge of the others. He then asked local white people to visit the Indians, read to them from the Bible, and teach them English. One volunteer was Harriet Beecher Stowe, the author of *Uncle Tom's Cabin.* The men embraced the changes and soon became model prisoners. Their enthusiasm inspired Pratt to send the youngest of them to school.

No institution would accept Indian warriors as students except Hampton Institute, which had been established a decade earlier to

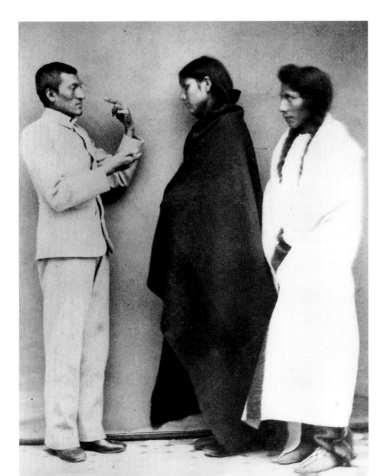

New students at Hampton, forbidden to speak their own languages, had to communicate by sign language until they learned English.
CUMBERLAND COUNTY HISTORICAL SOCIETY

educate emancipated slaves. Pratt sent seventeen prisoners to the Virginia school in the spring of 1878. Indians and African Americans attended Hampton together for the next forty years. Booker T. Washington, who became one of the nation's most prominent black leaders in the early twentieth century, was a supervisor of the Wigwam, the dormitory where Indian boys lived.

But Captain Pratt was unhappy with the conditions at the Virginia school. He worried that Indians at Hampton would become as segregated from white society as African Americans were at the time. So the captain persuaded the federal government to fund a school exclusively for Native Americans. Carlisle, with Pratt as superintendent, became the nation's most prominent Indian school and served as a model for other institutions. By the end of the century, the BIA had created twenty-five off-reservation boarding schools. It also opened dozens of schools on reservations. Some were boarding schools, where students lived in dormitories. Others were day schools, whose students lived at home. Captain Pratt disliked reservation schools, because it was too easy for students to see their families and friends and thus remain under the influence of the old ways.

At first many Native Americans fiercely opposed sending their children to any of the government schools. White authorities responded to their resistance with force and trickery. "Everything in the way of persuasion and argument having failed," reported one BIA agent, "it became necessary to visit the camp unexpectedly with a detachment of police, and seize such children as were proper and take them away to school, willing or unwilling."

The raid, this agent reported, threw the Indians into a panic.

One of the Bureau of Indian Affairs day schools on the Puget Sound in the Pacific Northwest. SMITHSONIAN INSTITUTION

Chilocco Indian Training School covered 8,000 acres of Oklahoma prairie. NATIONAL ARCHIVES

Parents "hurried their children off to the mountains or hid them away in camp, and the police had to chase and capture them like so many wild rabbits. This unusual proceeding created an outcry. The men were sullen and muttering, the women loud with lamentations, and the children almost out of their wits with fright."

There were many stories of youngsters who had been snatched up without warning. A Hopi boy left home one morning just as he had done for years and walked to his local reservation day school. The teacher put him and several other students into the back of a truck, enclosing them in a cage so they could not jump out and run away. The children were driven to a boarding school hundreds of miles away and did not see their homes again until years later.

Not every child had to be forced to attend school; some were eager to go. Gertrude Simmons's mother did not want her daughter to go far away to school. But Gertrude pleaded, "Oh mother, it is not that I wish to leave you, but I want to see the wonderful Eastern Land."

Other young Indians thought school would be easier than reservation life. "By the end of summer I had had enough of hoeing weeds and tending sheep," said Don Talayesva, a Hopi. "Helping my father was hard work, and I thought it was better to be educated."

When it became common for Indian children to go away to the military-style boarding schools, older children influenced the younger ones. "I remember when some of our boys came home from school back east, how nicely they were dressed in dark blue uniforms with yellow stripes on the arms and down the sides of their pants!" said a Pima boy. "I joined the others standing around admiring these boys' uniforms, and made up my mind that I would like to go to school too."

No matter how eager a child was to attend school, however, it was the rare boy or girl who did not feel lonely and scared in those first weeks away from home. Goes to War With described how she felt on her first day of school at Fort Defiance, near her reservation

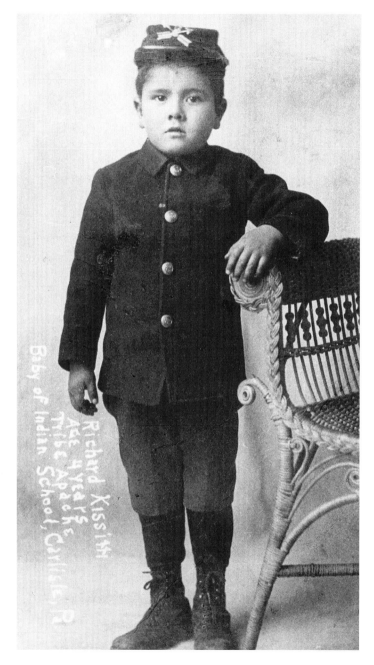

The boarding schools accepted very young students. This boy at Carlisle was only four years old.

*Shoshone and Arapaho students on their first day at Carlisle.
On the second day, after having their hair cut and exchanging
their reservation clothes for school clothing, they would look
very different.* CUMBERLAND COUNTY HISTORICAL SOCIETY

in the Canyon de Chelly region of Arizona: "All of a sudden I was
snatched away from those who loved and cared for me. This sudden change in my life was a shocking experience. From a primitive,
wild, Navajo life into a strange place with strange people, food,
clothing. I feared everything, especially the people and the strange
facilities."

4

FIRST DAYS AT SCHOOL

T HE FIRST DAYS OF SCHOOL are confusing for any child, but they were worse for Native Americans in the nineteenth century, who were thrust into a foreign world and stripped of their hair, their clothes, and even their names.

Soon after arriving at Carlisle in October 1879, the young Sioux had their first haircuts. Pratt allowed the older girls to keep their hair in braids, as they had done at home. But he trimmed the small girls' hair and cut the boys' hair short.

The haircuts were traumatic for many of the students. An older Carlisle boy who refused at first to have his hair cut walked outside his dormitory one night, took out a knife, and sliced off his long braids himself. He then began to wail, because the Sioux cut their hair only as a sign of sadness or shame. The students in nearby dormitories heard the wailing and joined in, as they would have done at home.

White people regarded long hair on men and boys as a sign of savagery, but Native Americans held different beliefs. "Our traditional hair was meaningful," a Hopi student explained. "The long hair we boys wore on the sides symbolized rain, you might say fertility, and it seemed to our parents that the whites were being pretty highhanded and insensitive as well as being ignorant of our ways."

Many of the young people fought having their hair cut. Gertrude hid under her bed, but was soon discovered. "I remem-

When the students first arrived, Captain Pratt often took photographs of them wearing traditional clothing. The students were photographed later, after they had been groomed and dressed like white people. Here is a Navajo student when he arrived, and the same young man three years later. ARMY WAR COLLEGE

ber being dragged out, though I resisted by kicking and scratching wildly," she said. "In spite of myself, I was carried downstairs and tied fast in a chair. I cried aloud, shaking my head all the while until I felt the cold blades of the scissors against my neck. . . . In my anguish I moaned for my mother, but no one came to comfort me."

A simple haircut at one reservation day school caused the building to empty faster than it did during a fire drill. Parents brought their children to the schoolhouse on the first day of class and then lingered outside, talking among themselves. The teachers had kept the barber's visit a secret. But one mother glanced through a window and saw a boy seated in a chair and, behind him, a man with scissors. A teacher described the pandemonium that followed: "Like a war whoop rang out the cry: 'Pabin Kaksa, Pabin Kaksa,' the enclosure rang with alarm, it invaded every room in the building and floated out on the prairie. No warning of fire or flood or tornado or hurricane, not even the approach of an enemy could have more effectively emptied the building as well as the grounds of the new school as did the ominous cry, 'They are cutting the hair.' Through doors and windows the children flew, down the steps, through the gates and over fences in a mad flight toward the Indian villages."

New students not only lost their long hair, they lost their clothing as well. In the early years of Indian education, before the white man's customs had been adopted on the reservations, boys and girls arrived at school wearing leggings, blankets, moccasins, and other traditional garments. But their clothes had to be discarded in exchange for trousers, dresses, and shoes.

"I was taken to a huge bathtub full of water," said Goes to War With, describing her first day at Fort Defiance Indian School. "I screamed and fought, but the big girl in charge was too strong. She got me in and scrubbed me. Then she put me into underwear and a dress with lots of buttons down the back. I remember how she combed my hair until it hurt. And the shoes she put on my feet were so strange and heavy. I was used to moccasins."

Ota Kte, however, was both pleased and puzzled by his new garments. "How proud we were with clothes that had pockets and boots that squeaked! We walked the floor nearly all that night. Many of the boys even went to bed with all of their clothes on. But in the morning the boys who had taken off their pants had a most

Boys, their hair already cut, taking baths on the first day at school.
SMITHSONIAN INSTITUTION

"Before" and "after" photographs of three Navajos, a girl and two boys.

terrible time. They did not know whether they were to button up in front or behind. Some of the boys said the open part went in front; others said, 'No it goes in back.' There is where the boys who had kept all their clothes on came in handy to look at. They showed the others that the pants buttoned up in front and not at the back."

Such confusion was at times embarrassing. In those days, men's pants had button flies instead of zippers. "A lot of us did not know how to work the buttons in front," recalled a Navajo boy, "and many just wet themselves."

Nearly as uncomfortable as new clothing were the new names. As one matron pointed out, teachers "would be at a disad-vantage in trying to be affectionate or disciplinary with an eight-syllabled girl like Sah-gah-ge-way-gah-bow-e-quay."

Not only were Indian names difficult to pronounce, but names such as Ota Kte, which translated as Plenty Kill, evoked a savage past. School officials assigned all of their students new names. Ota Kte's teachers at Carlisle gave him the first name of Luther and for a last name used the English translation of his father's name, Standing Bear.

A variety of methods were used to name students. "When you first started attending school, they looked at you, guessed how old you were, set your birthday, and gave you an age," Nakavoma remembered. "Then they'd assign you a Christian name. Mine turned out to be Fred." His last name, Kabotie, was a shortened form of his Hopi nickname.

At another school, students picked from a list written on a

Luther Standing Bear, standing in the middle, and his family.
CUMBERLAND COUNTY HISTORICAL SOCIETY

blackboard. Their new names were then printed on tags and sewn to their clothing to help everyone remember who was who. "When the teacher called the roll, no one answered his name," a student said. "Then she would walk around and look at the back of the boys' shirts. When she had the right name located, she made the boy stand up and say 'Present.' She kept this up for about a week before we knew what the sound of our new names was."

Some students were given odd names such as Rip Van Winkle and Julius Caesar. Most of the young Indians accepted whatever they were called, although a few did protest.

"I am going to tell you something about my name, Captain Pratt," complained a boy named Conrad. "I would like to have a

Apaches, who had been prisoners in Florida, on the day of their arrival at Carlisle, and again later. ABOVE: ARMY WAR COLLEGE; BELOW: CUMBERLAND COUNTY HISTORICAL SOCIETY

new name because some of the girls call me Cornbread and some call me Cornrat, so I do not like that name. So I want you to give me a new name. Now this is all I want to say."

Dressed in uncomfortable clothing and trying to remember their new names, the Indian students began to learn the white man's daily rituals. Even simple tasks like eating had to be relearned.

"One of the problems we faced was that we did not know how to eat at a table. We had to be told how to use the knife, fork, and spoon," one boy remembered. "We never used them at home, so we did not know what they were or how to use them, so we always wanted to stick our fingers in our food."

The young Indians also had to learn to eat unusual foods. "We ate bread and a thing called hash, which I did not like," said Don Talayesva. "It contained different kinds of food mixed together. Some were good and some were bad, but the bad outweighed the good. We also had prunes, rice, and tea. I had never tasted tea. The smell of it made me so sick that I thought I would vomit."

Another new feature of their lives was the rigid schedule. "We marched to the dining room three times a day to band music," one girl said, describing the students' daily routine at Phoenix Indian School. "We arose to a bell and had a given time for making our beds, cleaning our rooms, and being ready for breakfast. Everything was done on schedule, and there was no time for idleness."

The schools used military-style discipline, explained Samuel C. Armstrong, the superintendent of Hampton Institute, because it "enforces promptness, accuracy, and obedience, and goes further than any other influence could do to instill in the minds of the students what both Negro and Indian sadly lack, a knowledge of the value of time."

The officers were older students, and as Fred Kabotie explained, they took their responsibilities seriously. "Before breakfast we'd be out marching—left, left, left-right-left, and the captain would call out orders. 'Company, halt! Right face! About face!' If you didn't understand and obey quickly, he'd come around and kick you, so we learned fast."

After a few days at school, with their short hair and uniforms, the Indian students looked completely different. Their new look disturbed a delegation of Sioux who visited Carlisle in the spring of 1880. The visitors included Spotted Tail, White Thunder, and several other Sioux chiefs. They became angry when they saw their children dressed like soldiers and when they learned that the students were forbidden to speak their own language. The chiefs wanted to withdraw their sons and daughters from the school. But Captain Pratt persuaded all of them to change their minds except Spotted Tail, who took his children back to Rosebud.

Ernest White Thunder wanted desperately to return home with his father. Soon after arriving at school, the boy had become homesick. He was quiet and withdrawn and refused to participate in class or in other school activities. White Thunder told his unhappy son to work harder to learn English. Instead, Ernest sneaked onto the train the Sioux chiefs were riding back to the West. The boy was quickly discovered, and his father returned him to Carlisle.

Spotted Tail and a chief named Iron Wing photographed on their visit to Carlisle in the spring of 1880. CUMBERLAND COUNTY HISTORICAL SOCIETY

Ernest was so unhappy that he became ill. Captain Pratt feared the worst. "White Thunder's son is very sick and I doubt if he recovers," the superintendent wrote to one official. "I consider that it is entirely his own fault, as I explained to you. He is still rather obstinate—seems to rather want to die."

Just a few days later, Pratt had to send a sad letter to White Thunder. "Your son died quietly, without suffering, like a man. We

Ernest White Thunder was one of the many students who became ill and died. CUMBERLAND COUNTY HISTORICAL SOCIETY

have dressed him in his good clothes and tomorrow we will bury him the way the white people do."

It is hard to imagine dying of homesickness. Yet it was a very serious problem for Indian students. "Homesickness with them became a disease," wrote an official at Hampton Institute. "Boys and girls actually suffered in the flesh as well as the spirit; could not eat, would not sleep, and so prepared the way for serious trouble. When people do not take care of their bodies, it becomes easier for them to become sick."

The profound sadness caused by homesickness weakened the students and made them susceptible to deadly diseases such as tuberculosis and influenza. These contagious diseases easily spread because of unsanitary conditions at the boarding schools. It was not unusual for dozens of students to sleep in one big room lined with rows of beds or for two children to sleep together in a single bed. This enabled germs to spread easily from child to child.

An alarming number of young people died at the boarding schools. The Spokanes, a tribe from the region that is now Washington State, sent twenty-one children away to school; sixteen of them died there. At the Fort Hall School in Idaho, sixty-eight students caught scarlet fever. Eight of them died quickly, and another thirty became so ill they were sent home to die. Officials usually returned the sickest children to their parents so their deaths would not reflect badly on the schools. Nonetheless, so many students died that each institution had its own cemetery. This high death rate was one reason that parents refused to send their children away to school.

Most BIA schools had their own cemeteries because so many students died. This is the cemetery at Carlisle. CUMBERLAND COUNTY HISTORICAL SOCIETY

Not all young Indians who were unhappy became depressed or sick. Some expressed their unhappiness in a healthier manner—by rebelling.

Many students rebelled by running away from school. The problem was particularly bad in the first few weeks of school, when dozens of homesick children typically fled. Running away was dangerous. Three boys fled from the Cheyenne River School one winter. Two were found alive, but the third, Pius Little Bear, froze to death. A few children ran away and were never heard from again, by either their teachers or their parents.

At Fort Mojave School in Arizona, some of the worst truants were only seven and eight years old. After locking up several run-aways, one teacher recalled, she heard the loud sound of smashing wood. She went to investigate. "At the sturdy jail, there lay the sturdy door, broken from its hinges. There lay the log, a big one, and the many pieces of rope. We were amazed." The children had made handles from the rope and used the log as a battering ram to break down the jail door and free those inside.

Students sometimes expressed their unhappiness violently. Two Carlisle girls tried to burn down their dormitory. They set newspapers on fire in the reading room and then hurried to join the other pupils at dinner. The blaze was quickly discovered and extinguished. Later that day, the two arsonists tried again. They filled a pillowcase with paper, lit it, and tossed the flaming bundle into a closet. This blaze was also quickly discovered and put out. Fellow students knew who had started the fire and forced the girls to confess. The pair were arrested, tried, and sentenced to eighteen months in the Pennsylvania women's penitentiary.

Indian school officials disciplined students in many different ways. Teachers often used shame or embarrassment as punishment. A boy caught sneaking food out of the dining room had to stand on a chair in the middle of the room during dinner. A girl who wet her bed had to carry a mattress for a day. Punishment was not always fair. When Fred Kabotie played hooky from the reservation day school he attended before going away to boarding school, the teacher made his sister stand for hours with her nose pressed against a circle on the blackboard.

BIA regulations forbade harsh punishment, but these rules were ignored. Schools had a faculty member called the disciplinarian, who was usually a man strong enough to whip or paddle older boys. Many schools locked students in a guardhouse for several days or even weeks for serious infractions such as fighting, drinking alcohol, and running away.

Another punishment was hard labor. "If you had done something extremely out of line, you worked on the rock pile on Saturday," one boy said of the dreaded sentence. "You went down there and took a sledgehammer and made little ones out of big ones so they could get 'em down to the size to get 'em in the rock crusher. That was brutal work—it was like being in prison."

Disciplining Indians who were old enough to be warriors was not always easy. Once Captain Pratt summoned a young man to his office for arguing with a teacher. Pratt locked his office door and picked up a leather strap. The student grabbed the strap and warned, "If you think you can whip me, you are *muy loco*. Nobody has ever struck me in all my life, and nobody ever will. I could break your neck with my bare hands."

Students eventually learned to express their unhappiness in ways that were acceptable to their white teachers. A boy named Rip Van Winkle, who had been whisked away four years earlier to school in Colorado, wrote a letter to the BIA agent who was in charge of his reservation in Arizona. "I am getting tired of this place and want to come home this summer," the student wrote.

"Most all of the Navajo boys want to go home to see their people. They are anxious to go home." The letter persuaded authorities to let the boy return to his family.

Rip Van Winkle's request showed that young Indians were learning the white man's way. Instead of running away or trying to burn down their dormitories, they began to address their grievances to the proper officials.

In the early days of the boarding schools unhappiness and rebellion were intensified because the Native American students could not speak English and therefore could not make their feelings known. The new pupils' first assignment was to learn "the white man's tongue."

5

LEARNING THE WHITE MAN'S WAY

"A CLASS OF BOYS AND GIRLS ignorant of every rule of school or society sits mute before you. You smile and say 'Good Morning,' they return the smile in a hopeless kind of way, but not the 'Good Morning.' By a series of homemade signs, which they are quick to interpret, they are made to understand that they are to repeat your greeting, and you are rewarded with a gruff or timid 'Good Monink,' and thus another gate is open to the 'white man's road.'"

As this teacher's account suggests, most of the Native American students did not understand or speak English. Carlisle's instructors taught the language using a text called *First Lessons for the Deaf and Dumb*. The book advised filling the classroom with everyday items such as furniture, clothing, tools, and food. The teacher then wrote the names of these objects on the blackboard and the pupils copied them. The instructor walked from desk to desk, stopping frequently to guide a student's hand as he or she painstakingly formed each letter. Then the class practiced speaking the strange words. "At first I was unable to make many sounds," one boy said. "I even had trouble pronouncing the letters of the alphabet. It didn't seem like I would ever learn."

Ohiyesa, whose name had been changed to Charles Eastman, described his frustration in learning English: "For a whole week we youthful warriors were held up and harassed with words of those

Classwork was kept simple until students learned English. Notice the day's lesson written on the blackboard: Conversation Lesson Subject—The Chair. ARMY WAR COLLEGE

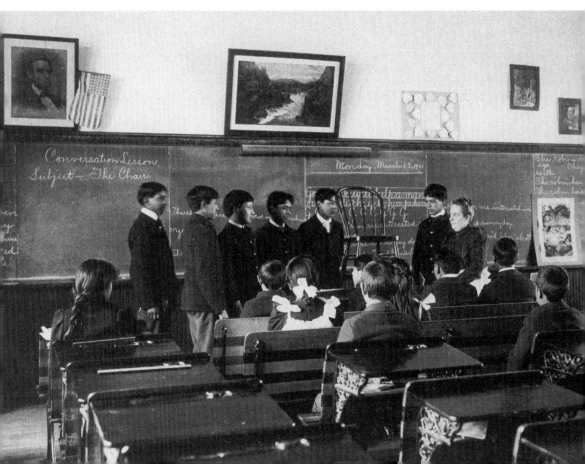

apple   get   they   all

apples   grew   apple   get

green   all   grew   how

Frank   grow   give   trees

Frank is in the apple tree.

he has an apple in his hand.

it is a large red apple.

he will give it to Ann.

Carlisle Barracks Pa.

June 25: 1880

My dear father

I am going to write to you this afternoon
this here at Carlisle all the boys and girls
like very nice school some boys
and girls read in book every day work
hard.   good by

From your son

Rutherford B. Hayes.

+3 −4 + 1×2 = 14

from 3 0 2
take 1 1 8
rem. 1 8 4

John Williams

Choate. Photographer

A writing slate prepared by a student whose new name was the
same as a former U.S. President, Rutherford B. Hayes.

letters. Like raspberry bushes in the path, they tore, bled, and sweated us—those little words like *rat, eat,* and so forth—until not a semblance of our native dignity and self-respect was left."

The Indian students had to study English for a year or more before they knew enough to begin studying subjects such as math, art, hygiene, and history. While learning the language of white

Two boys studying in their dorm room. ARMY WAR COLLEGE

people, the youngsters were often surprised by how differently they viewed the world.

"We had to learn that clocks had something to do with the hours and minutes that the white people mentioned so often," an Arapaho girl explained when she first learned about the white man's concept of time. "Hours, minutes, and seconds were such small divisions of time that we had never thought of them. When the sun rose, when it was high in the sky, and when it set were all the divisions of the day that we had ever found necessary when we followed the old Arapaho road. When we went on the hunting trip or to a sun dance, we counted time by sleeps."

One of the main lessons taught in every class was that the white man's way of life was superior to all others. One student expressed what he had learned in an essay:

"The white people they are civilized. They have everything and go to school, too. They learn how to read and write so they can read newspaper.

"The yellow people they half civilized, some of them know how to read and write, and some know how to half take care of themself.

"The red people they big savages; they don't know nothing."

The teachers who taught these lessons often felt as though they were on a mission to solve the "Indian problem," to convert savages into model citizens. Many instructors were women, who had few other career choices. Their salaries were low and the schools they taught in were in remote parts of the West. They often worked with colleagues who had little training or interest in

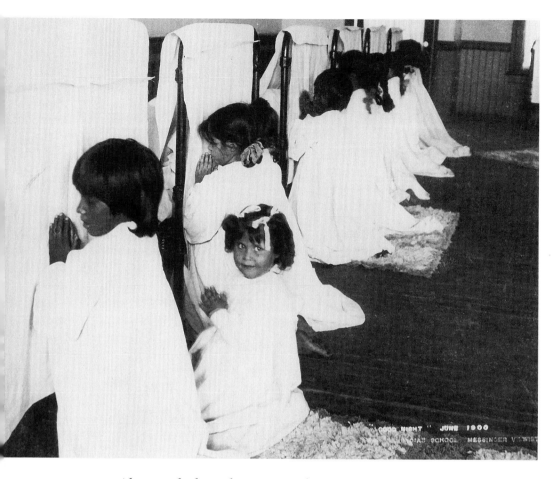

*Along with their classroom and vocational work, students were
taught Christianity.* NATIONAL ARCHIVES

teaching. The students gave incompetent or unpopular instructors
nicknames like Billy Goat and The Woman Who Makes You
Scream. However, they readily recognized good teachers. "She was
not bossy like most white ladies are," one boy said of a favorite
teacher. "She seemed to know without being told that I wanted
desperately to be able to read, and she helped me."

Some staff members profoundly influenced their pupils' lives.

The Sante Fe School superintendent, John De Huff, and his wife, Elizabeth, noticed that Fred Kabotie was good at drawing. Mrs. De Huff asked Fred's teacher to excuse him from shop class so that he could go to her home. The two of them would drink tea and eat cookies together, and then Mrs. De Huff would give the boy drawing paper and watercolors so he could spend the afternoon painting. After years of encouragement and practice, Fred Kabotie

Carlisle's teachers and staff. Captain Pratt is the tall man standing in the middle. ARMY WAR COLLEGE

became a famous artist whose work was sold in the United States and in Europe.

At Hampton Institute, the school physician befriended an Omaha student named Susan La Flesche. The doctor, a woman, encouraged the girl's ambition to go into medicine. At that time, very few women went to medical school. La Flesche graduated class salutatorian in 1886 and then attended medical school in Philadelphia, where she earned her degree in just three years. She was the first Native American woman to become a doctor, and she was one of the few women doctors in the country. La Flesche returned home to Nebraska, where she became the principal physician on the Omaha Reservation.

Not all whites were as supportive as these staff members. Few white people believed that Native Americans were capable of being doctors or artists. "The Indian is an adult child," claimed Francis Leupp, who was the commissioner of Indian affairs in the early twentieth century. "He has the physical attributes of the adult with the mentality of about our fourteen-year-old boy." Because of this attitude, the schools stressed vocational training. Students spent half a day studying English, arithmetic, and other academic subjects. The rest of the day they worked at a job.

Student labor was essential on every boarding school campus. Carlisle, the largest of the institutions, grew rapidly. By the turn of the century, it had forty-nine buildings, over half of them built by student carpenters and bricklayers. The boys also ran the school's three-hundred-acre farm, caring for cows, horses, chickens, and pigs as well as plowing, planting, and harvesting crops.

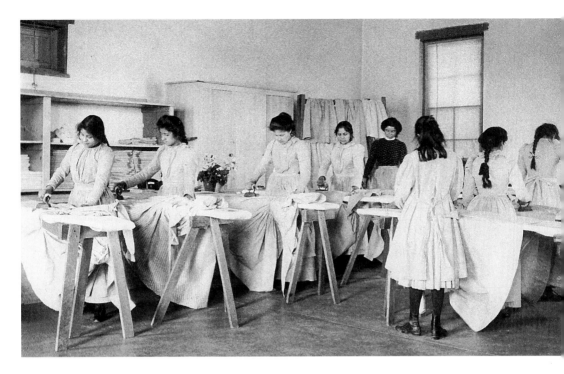

Indian girls ironing school laundry. ARMY WAR COLLEGE

The girls cooked and cleaned. Irene Stewart, the former Goes to War With, described some of the many jobs that girls of all ages performed. "We were detailed to work in the laundry and do all the washing for the school, the hospital, and the sanitarium. Sewing was hard, too. We learned to sew all clothing, except underwear and stockings, and we learned to mend and darn and patch. We canned food, cooked, washed dishes, waited on tables, scrubbed floors, and washed windows. We cleaned classrooms and dormitories. By the time I graduated from the sixth grade, I was a well-trained worker."

The long hours of hard work left bitter memories. "I have never forgotten how the steam in the laundry made me sick; how standing and ironing for hours made my legs ache far into the night," Stewart said. "By evening I was too tired to play and just fell asleep wherever I sat down. I think this is why the boys and girls ran away from school, why some became ill, why it was so hard to learn. We were too tired to study."

Whether students liked their jobs or not, one girl who cleaned explained, they had to work; otherwise, they were punished. "If you were not finished when the 8 A.M. whistle sounded, the dining room matron would go around strapping us while we were still on our hands and knees. This was just the right position for a swat—all the matron had to do was raise our dresses and strap."

The work was not all drudgery. Some students actually enjoyed their tasks. "I loved being on the farm, outdoors all day, and I worked at everything," Fred Kabotie said of his chores at the Sante Fe School. "The cows had to be milked at four in the morning and again in the afternoon, and the milk delivered to the kitchen. During the day I'd be feeding poultry, or out in the fields hoeing, or feeding the pigs with my friend Joe, the horse."

The students also enjoyed the wages they earned for their work. Most of their earnings were deposited into a bank account until they left school, but they were given some spending money. "The dollar paid me was a small fortune," an Iroquois girl said, recalling her Saturday trips to a snack bar, "and I would make it stretch to at least four trips to the Shack."

Many of the school jobs were intended to teach students skills they would need to live in the white man's world. The training for girls was limited, because in those days people felt women were

All students had to work on the school farms raising livestock and vegetables. CUMBERLAND COUNTY HISTORICAL SOCIETY

best suited to be mothers and homemakers. Indian girls learned only to cook, sew, and clean. Boys learned a variety of trades, such as farming, butchering, tinsmithing, tailoring, shoemaking, painting, glazing, brickmaking, printing, and wagon-making.

The schools trained their students well, and their work was in demand. Carlisle's printers produced thousands of forms for government offices in Washington, D.C. At the Chilocco Indian School in northern Oklahoma, student farmers raised prizewinning livestock. And in Phoenix, Indian schoolgirls were popular maids for white people's homes.

Indian boys training to be shoemakers. ARMY WAR COLLEGE

The school also provided practical work experience, called the "outing" program. It was Captain Pratt's idea to send students to live for a year with a white farm family. The Indian boys and girls attended local schools and churches while helping the host families with farmwork or housework. Before their "outing," students had to know basic English. They also had to promise to obey their hosts, bathe regularly, attend church, and avoid drinking,

CARLISLE INDIAN SCHOOL

CARLISLE, PENNSYLVANIA _____ _Nov._ _8_ _____ 190 _0_

M. FRIEDMAN, SUPT.
    Sir:
    I want to go out into the country.
    If you will send me I promise to OBEY MY EMPLOYER, TO KEEP ALL THE RULES OF THE SCHOOL.
    I will attend Sunday School and Church regularly.
    I will not absent myself from my farm home without permission of my employer and will not loaf about stores or elsewhere evenings or Sundays.
    I will not make a practice of staying for meals when I visit my friends.
    I will not use tobacco nor any spirituous liquors in any form.
    I will not play cards nor gamble, and will save as much money as possible.
    If out for the winter I will attend school regularly and will do my best to advance myself in my studies.
    I will bathe regularly, write my home letter every month, and do all that I can to please my employer, improve myself and make the best use of the chance given me.   Very respectfully,

_____ _Alice M Bellanger_, Pupil.

NOTE:—This request is to be signed in triplicate, one copy to be kept by pupil, one retained in Superintendent's office, and one sent to employer.

Boarding school students had to promise, in writing, to be extra good when they went on their year "outing" with a white family.

gambling, and smoking. The white families sent the school monthly reports on the students' behavior.

Outing worked well on the farms in Pennsylvania, but it was not successful in the West, where most of the Indian schools were located. Chilocco's superintendent said he visited "several farmers to try to arrange for work for the Indian boys. In some cases, we were rebuffed quite harshly." The memory of frontier hostilities was still fresh, and white people refused to hire Native Americans for anything except the most menial jobs.

Although Indian students spent long hours in classes and at work, they did find time for friends, mischief, and even romance.

6

PARCHED CORN SOCIETIES
AND SATURDAY SOCIALS

Though they were immersed in the white man's world, the Native American students did not immediately forget their heritage. Groups of boys at Chilocco, who jokingly called themselves "parched corn societies," would steal away in the late afternoons to meeting places in a distant grove of trees.

"They'd go out and build a fire and parch corn," one of the boys said of those evenings, "and then they'd make little tom-toms out of tin cans with rubber stretched over the top, and they'd have stomp dances around those fires at night, and it was a lot of fun."

Other parts of the Indian heritage were more troublesome. "Till I arrived at school," one student said, "I had never heard that there were any other Indians in the country other than those of our reservation." As many as seventy different tribes were represented at the largest institutions. They included Apaches from the Southwest, Crows from the western plains, and even Eskimos from the above Arctic Circle.

Eskimos were among the thousands of Native Americans who attended BIA boarding schools. ARMY WAR COLLEGE

Some of these tribes had been enemies for generations, a fact few students forgot. Luther Standing Bear met a Pawnee boy whom he had seen a few years earlier as a Sioux prisoner. They did not renew old animosities, but they did not become friends either. Don Talayesva remembered how he and his friends picked on a little boy by jerking his ears: "We Hopis hated Navajos and decided to make this one miserable."

Many of the young people learned to overlook traditional antagonisms. "There were certain tribes that were clannish," a student explained, "that ran around together strictly because they belonged to the same tribe. That wasn't much true generally. I think all the students were pretty much thrown together. . . . Your friends, naturally, were the ones in your own age group, and of course later on the ones you worked with."

But another division, which had not been a problem in the old days, developed. Full-blooded Indians felt superior to those who had a white parent or grandparent. One boy described his reaction when the other kids called him *stahitkey,* or "white man." "There was nothing more despicable than to be called a white man," he said. "I had many, many fights over the fact that I was fair-skinned."

Students did not always get along with one another, but they usually united against their teachers. A boy who enjoyed fooling adults remembered changing the words to the hymns he was taught by missionaries. "Always we'd sing the same songs, over and over. And I used to think, 'My goodness, these Christians never have any new songs.' It gets monotonous. . . . We enjoyed it anyway, because we'd sing Hopi words to 'Jesus loves me, this I know' that sounded like the English but had funny meanings."

The same boy remembered an instructor who punished tardy students by lining them up and giving them several whacks with a paddle. "We'd pass the word in Hopi, 'When he hits you, start crying. Then he'll leave you alone.'"

After a few years, the Indians began to resemble their counterparts in any American school, spending their spare time with friends, talking about clothes and the opposite sex.

One girl described how she and her friends spent their

Indian students, like this boy in a canoe, learned to spend their free time like other American young people. ARMY WAR COLLEGE

evenings in the dormitory sewing clothes, fixing their hair, playing cards, singing, and dancing together. "There wasn't much to do, but that's what you did. If you ran out of that, then you got your [school] books out."

Boys as well as girls were concerned with being in style. "Tailormade trousers were the in thing at Chilocco at that time," a teenager explained. "There was a tailor in town that would make you [trousers] and they all had to have twenty-two-inch bottoms—

Boys reading and playing checkers in a dormitory reading room at Hampton Institute. HAMPTON UNIVERSITY ARCHIVES

they called them bell-bottoms. That was the in thing. If you had a pair of twenty-two-inch tailormade bell-bottom trousers, that was the ultimate at Chilocco."

Dormitory matrons kept close watch over the girls, who were not allowed to be near boys except during meals, in class, and at weekend socials. "You could not even talk to your sister," a boy complained, "without going to the principal and making special arrangements. You even had to prove she was your sister."

Despite rigid rules, romances did develop. Anna Moore, a

Pima girl, met her future husband, Ross Shaw, when she was a fourteen-year-old student at the Phoenix School. "We wrote notes, because the matron was very strict and only let us see each other at social functions," she explained. "But sometimes Ross would sneak over to the girls' side of the campus, where we would play croquet until the matron discovered us and shooed Ross back where he belonged."

The schools held socials for older boys and girls on Saturday

On weekends, boarding school students shed their uniforms in favor of civilian clothes. Even during free time, boys and girls were kept apart. LIBRARY OF CONGRESS

nights, when they gathered in the dining hall to play checkers, work puzzles, blow bubbles, and toss beanbags. Some Saturdays they held dances. Dressed up in their best clothes, the students self-consciously danced the two-step, the waltz, and the Virginia reel. Teachers watched to make sure they did not dance too closely and that boys did not put their hands in the wrong place. "You had to be held a certain way," one girl said. "The boys weren't allowed to put their hands high on you or low on you."

These dances were nerve-racking affairs for many students. Jim Whitewolf, a Kiowa Apache who attended Chilocco, vividly described a Saturday night dance. The girls had invited the boys anonymously. Whitewolf suspected that his invitation had come from a Comanche girl who had sent him a note two weeks earlier, asking him to be her sweetheart. The teenager had been too shy to reply.

On Saturday, while taking a bath, putting on his best clothes, and polishing his shoes, Whitewolf became more and more nervous as he wondered whom he would meet that night. He described how he felt at the dance:

"We had hair oil on our hair, and we had flowers in our but-tonholes, handkerchiefs in our pockets, and our neckties were all tied. All of us boys marched in by twos. We stood real straight and had our coats buttoned up. . . . Pretty soon, as we were sitting, all the girls came in dressed in white, with red flowers on. They were sure pretty. My heart was just shaking. I didn't know which was the girl who had invited me. The girls knew whom they had invited, and they each sat down beside the boy they invited. A girl came over and sat down by me. I just sat there real straight. It was the Comanche girl who had written me that note before."

School authorities tried very hard to keep boys and girls from being alone together. Ignoring the possibility of fire, some officials bolted the doors and nailed the windows shut in the girls' dormitory.

Although sex was strictly forbidden, it did happen occasionally.

Student officers at Hampton Institute. HAMPTON UNIVERSITY ARCHIVES

One boy recalled that late at night the girls hung sheets from their dormitory windows to pull up the boys. Girls who became pregnant were pressured to get married or were sent home. Officials rarely recorded these pregnancies, because they reflected badly on the institutions.

Teachers encouraged students to be involved in extracurricular activities, and many Indian boys and girls participated enthusiasti-

Members of a literary club at Hampton. HAMPTON UNIVERSITY ARCHIVES

cally. The Bush-misters drill team was an elite campus organization at the Phoenix school. Joining or being elected an officer in the Bush-misters enhanced a student's status. Good drill teams and bands created favorable attention for the Indian schools. The Carlisle band played to tens of thousands of spectators at parades in Washington, D.C., and New York City. But the activity that brought the most attention to Indian schools was sports.

7

POP WARNER'S REDMEN

I N THE FALL OF 1893, forty Carlisle schoolboys visited Captain
Pratt in his office. The superintendent knew they had something important to say. The boys who had gathered by the office
door were the school's best athletes, and the one doing all the talking was Carlisle's champion debater.

He asked the captain to allow the boys to play football. Pratt
had disbanded the school team the previous year, after a player
had broken his leg in a game against nearby Dickinson College.
Impressed by the students' desire to play the sport, Pratt agreed to
let them organize a team. "If, through football, Indian boys can
kick themselves into association and competition with white
people," he explained, "I would give everyone a football." This
decision, so casually made, proved to be monumental for Carlisle.

Many Indian schools had trophy-winning teams and athletes.
Chilocco's amateur boxers regularly fought in national champion-

ship matches at New York City's Madison Square Garden. Riverside in California, Haskell in Kansas, and Phoenix in Arizona won state titles in track, football, and baseball. But no other Indian school achieved as much athletic fame as Carlisle.

In the first decade of the twentieth century, the Pennsylvania school was known across the nation for its outstanding football teams, track stars, and baseball players. One star baseball player was Albert "Chief" Bender, who went on to become an outstanding pitcher for the Philadelphia Athletics and was later voted into baseball's Hall of Fame. Another notable athlete was the runner Louis Tewanima, a silver-medal winner in the 1912 Olympics. Like many other Hopi boys, Tewanima had been trained as a long-distance runner to deliver messages between distant tribal villages.

Two of the most famous men in American sports made their reputations at the Pennsylvania Indian school. They were Glenn Scobey "Pop" Warner and Jim Thorpe. Pop Warner, a white man, was an innovative coach in the early days of football. He is credited with introducing the screen pass, the single-wing and double-wing formations, and the practice of identifying each play by a number.

Warner coached at Carlisle for eleven years. He believed that Indians were good athletes because they tended to be exceptionally patient and persistent. Also, the coach often said, his players had something to prove:

"When playing against college teams it was not to them so much Carlisle School against Pennsylvania or Harvard, as the case might be, but it was the Indian against the White Man. . . . It was not that they felt any definite bitterness against the conquering white, or against the government for years of unfair treatment, but rather that they believed the armed contests between red men and white had never been waged on equal terms."

Carlisle became a national football powerhouse. Pop Warner scheduled his games in cities where they could draw large crowds. As many as thirty thousand fans filled the stadiums when the team—dressed in the school colors, gold and red—visited Boston to play Harvard College or New York to play West Point. The spectators enjoyed pointing out players named Afraid of Bear, Tomahawk, or Bravethunder.

Warner coached many good athletes, but Jim Thorpe was the only one he called a "natural-born football player." Thorpe grew up on the Sac and Fox reservation in northern Oklahoma, where hard physical play was a natural part of childhood. "Our favorite game was 'follow the leader,'" Thorpe said. "Depending on the leader, that can be made an exciting game. Many times in following I had to swim rivers, climb trees, and run under horses."

In 1904, at age sixteen, Thorpe enrolled at Carlisle. Although he had attended two other schools, the teenager had never played organized sports. On his way to a game of sandlot football, he walked across the track field, where several boys were practicing the high jump.

"I stopped to watch them as they went higher and higher," he explained. "After a while they had the bar set at five feet nine inches, and none of them could jump over it. They were just about ready to call it a day when I asked if I might try it.

Jim Thorpe, left, in the lead during a high hurdles race. ARMY WAR COLLEGE

"I had a pair of overalls on, a hickory shirt, and a pair of gymnasium shoes I had picked up in the gym that belonged to someone else. I looked like anything but a high jumper. The track athletes snickered a bit as the bar was set up for me. I cleared the bar on my first try." The jump impressed Coach Warner, who told Thorpe to come to practice the next day dressed appropriately in shorts and running shoes.

Thorpe excelled at track and field. He participated in the 1912 Summer Olympics in Stockholm, where he won two gold medals. One medal was for the pentathlon, which consisted of the broad jump, javelin throw, 200-meter run, discus throw, and 1500-meter run. Thorpe won four of these five events. His second gold medal was for winning the decathlon, which consisted of the 100-meter dash, 10-pound shot put, high jump, half-mile walk, hammer throw, pole vault, high hurdles, 50-pound weight throw, broad jump, and the mile run. Thorpe won six of these ten events.

At the Olympic awards ceremony, Thorpe made a comment that was talked about nearly as much as his athletic feats. The king of Sweden presented the medals, shook Thorpe's hand, and said, "Sir, you are the greatest athlete in the world." Thorpe acknowledged the compliment with a simple "Thanks, King."

The young man's Olympic performance was marred a year later when a sportswriter discovered that the all-round athlete had played semi-professional baseball one summer. At the time, only amateurs were eligible to compete in the Olympic Games. Olympic officials stripped the track star of his medals. Seventy years later, long after Thorpe's death, the medals were restored.

Even before his Olympic achievements, Thorpe had come to national prominence as a gridiron star. He was named All-American in two of the four years he played football at Carlisle. His last season, 1912, was one of Carlisle's best. The team that year seemed invincible as it compiled a record of one-sided victories. It beat Villanova, 65–0, Syracuse, 33–0, the University of Pittsburgh, 45–8, and Brown, 32–0.

One of the team's biggest games was against West Point. Before they took the field, the quarterback recalled, Pop Warner "had no trouble getting the boys keyed up for the game. He

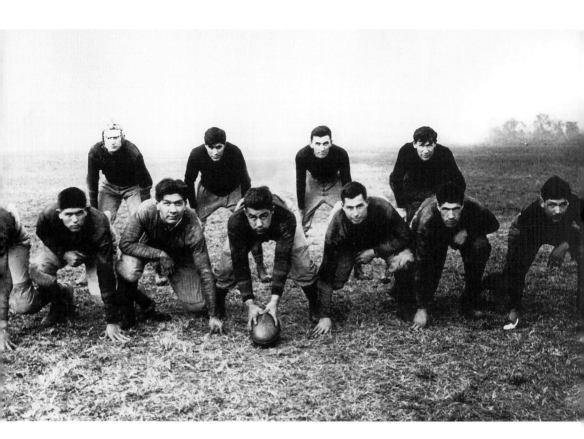

Carlisle's football team in 1912. Jim Thorpe is in the back row on the far right. ARMY WAR COLLEGE

reminded the boys that it was the fathers and grandfathers of these army players who fought the Indians. That was enough."

The headline in the *New York Times* read, "Thorpe's Indians Crush West Point: Brilliancy of Carlisle Redskin's Play Amazes Cadets and Spectators." Carlisle won, 27–6.

One cadet was a halfback named Dwight D. Eisenhower. Forty years later, he was elected president of the United States. "On the football field, there was no one like him in the world," Eisenhower said of Thorpe. "Against us, he dominated all of the action."

THE FOOTBALL TRAIL OF GLORY

1912 SUMMARY

Date	Opponent	Where	Ind.	Opp.
Sept. 21	Albright College	Carlisle, Pa.	50	7
Sept. 25	Lebanon Valley Coll.	Carlisle, Pa.	45	0
Sept. 28	Dickinson College	Carlisle, Pa.	34	0
Oct. 2	Villanova College	Harrisburg, Pa.	65	0
Oct. 5	Washington & Jefferson College	Washington, Pa.	0	0
Oct. 12	Syracuse Univ.	Syracuse, N.Y.	33	0
Oct. 19	Univ. of Pittsburgh	Pittsburgh, Pa.	45	8
Oct. 26	Georgetown Univ.	Washington, D.C.	34	20
Oct. 28	Toronto Univ.	Toronto, Canada	49	1
Nov. 2	Lehigh Univ.	S. Bethlehem, Pa.	34	14
Nov. 9	Army	West Point. N.Y.	27	6
Nov. 16	Univ. of Pennsylvania	Philadelphia, Pa.	26	34
Nov. 23	Springfield Train. Sch.	Springfield, Mass.	30	24
Nov. 28	Brown Univ.	Providence, R.I.	32	0
			504	114

Won 12; Lost 1; Tied 1

Carlisle's football record for the 1912 season.

The Indians finished the season with twelve wins, one tie, and one loss. They led the nation in scoring. In fourteen games, their opponents scored only 114 points, whereas Carlisle scored 504 points. Thorpe scored 198 of them.

When the team returned to Carlisle, hundreds of students met the players at the train station, and they all paraded through town together. Sports were important to the young people.

"The thing that pulled me through was the athletic training at Carlisle," said one man. "We had the world beat." Another student, in a letter home, boasted that his school had trounced the much bigger University of Pittsburgh in a football game. "Maybe white men better with cannon and guns," the boy observed in his still imperfect English, "but Indian just as good in brains to think with."

8

BLANKET INDIANS AND RED PROGRESSIVES

GRADUATION DAY AT THE BOARDING SCHOOLS gave students a chance to display their progress toward "civilization." Young orators gave speeches with such titles as "The Value of Domestic Training" and "Christianity and the Indian." In the classrooms, students exhibited handmade crocheted placemats and leather harnesses. Parents, faculty, and townspeople gathered at the parade grounds to hear the school bands play John Philip Sousa's marching music and to watch the drill teams' precise routines.

The graduation ceremonies also gave school officials one last chance to urge students to forget their tribal past. "Let all that is Indian within you die!" declared one speaker. "You cannot become truly American citizens, industrious, intelligent, cultured, civilized, until the Indian within you is dead."

Yet beneath the festive atmosphere and optimistic speeches lurked a troubling question: How many of the young men and

Carlisle's graduating class of 1897. ARMY WAR COLLEGE

women would stay on the white man's road? "Think of all of the temptations and influence of my people I have to face," observed a Kiowa girl. "This is the commencement of a hard life for me."

Most graduates returned to their reservations to live among family, friends, and familiar ways. But it was not easy to go back home.

As soon as Polingaysi Qoyawayma returned to her Hopi village from Sherman Indian High School in California, she began criti-

Graduation Exercises

卐

Thursday Afternoon, April 2, 1908

1:15 o'clock

卐

INVOCATION	REV. G. M. DIFFENDERFER
	Chaplain
OVERTURE—"ORPHEUS"—*Offenbach*	School Band
INDUSTRIAL TALK—"BANDAGING"	ELIZABETH BAIRD
	(Oneida)
INDUSTRIAL TALK—"MY PLANS FOR DEVELOPING MY ALLOTMENT"	
	THOMAS EAGELMAN
	(Sioux)
CLASS EXERCISE—"SWEEPING AND DUSTING"	NORMAL PUPILS
	UNDER VERA WAGNER
	(Alaskan)
INDUSTRIAL TALK—"MY PEOPLE"	ELIZABETH PENNY
	(Nez Perce)
INDUSTRIAL TALK—"CARPENTERING"	JOHN FAHR
	(Chippewa)
GRADUATION SONG	THE GRADUATING CLASS
RECITATION—"THE PEACE PIPE"	ALICE DENOMIE
	(Chippewa)
SECLECTION—"THE TATTOOED MAN"—*Herbert*	School Band
ADDRESS AND PRESENTATION OF DIPLOMAS	
	HON. M. E. OLMSTEAD, M.C.
SONG—"AMERICA"	AUDIENCE
BENEDICTION	REV. DR. H. G. GANSS
	Chaplain

卐

Note—The audience will kindly remain until the students march out.

A graduation program from 1908. The swastika, similar to those on the program, is best known today as an emblem for Nazi Germany. Before the Nazis adopted the swastika in the 1920s, it was an ancient symbol of good luck common in Native American and other cultures worldwide.

cizing her parents: "Why haven't you bought a white man's bed to sleep on? And a table? You should not be eating on the floor as the Old Ones did. When I was a little girl, I did not mind sleeping on the floor and eating from a single bowl into which everyone dipped. But I am used to another way of living now, and I do not intend to do these things." Her parents did not like to be lectured to by their daughter. No one was happy. The young woman soon moved away to live with white missionaries.

Many returning students were met with hostility. "If you minded your own business and tried to live in the white man's way," said Jason Betzinez, "then the Indians branded you as being some kind of an outcast who no longer loved his own people."

On every reservation there was a group devoted to the old ways. These people were called traditionalists, or blanket Indians. Former students who joined this group were said to have "returned to the blanket." The traditionalists pressured young men and women to embrace the ways of their ancestors.

The pressure often came from the students' families. After Don Talayesva moved back to his Hopi village, his parents, grandparents, and other relatives urged him to join the Wowochim religious society. "I knew that it was an important rule for boys to take this important step into manhood," Talayesva said. "Some of my uncles had told me that if I were not initiated, the people would call me boy all my life . . . the girls would not regard me as a man . . . all of my uncles and relatives would be against me." He soon gave in and rejected white culture completely.

It was not only pressure from family and friends that forced

Former Indian school students back home on the reservation.
HAMPTON UNIVERSITY ARCHIVES

young Indians to return to the blanket. Reservations were ghettos, isolated and poor. They often were distant from cities and towns. And even when towns were nearby, white hostility kept Native Americans away. Jobs were scarce. Former students quickly discovered that there was little use for the dressmaking or tinsmithing skills they had learned at school.

One Carlisle graduate wrote a letter that expressed his unhappiness to Captain Pratt. "I have not tools to work with, or plows to work the ground to make corn. Can you send me some? I am again a Comanche. I was compelled to go back to the old road, though I did not want to, but I had no pants and had to take leggings. I never have any money, for I cannot earn it here. . . . Now when I want to work the white man's road and learn it, I have nothing to do it with."

Some Native Americans became especially bitter toward their alma maters. A Carlisle graduate named Plenty Horses murdered an army lieutenant in 1891 at Pine Ridge, South Dakota. Plenty Horses said he killed the man to remove the stain of Carlisle's influence.

So many former students returned to the blanket that critics claimed the BIA schools were failing. "Go to Pine Ridge or Rosebud," one politician complained about the Sioux reservations in South Dakota, "and select from the thousands the most gaudily dressed of the young savages, those whose faces are continually smeared with paint, whose feet now know no covering but heavily beaded moccasins, those whose blankets are decorated to excess, and you will discover a Carlisle or Hampton boy."

But most Indian school alumni, even those who were successful in the white man's world, embraced their Native American heritage. Fred Kapotie explained how his Hopi background shaped his art: "I started painting things I remembered from home, mostly kachinas. When you're so remote from your own people, you get lonesome. You don't paint what's around you, you paint what you have in mind. Loneliness moves you to express something of your home, your background."

Indian school graduates who returned to their reservations

often became tribal leaders. For the first time in many tribes, the new generation of leaders included women. The first woman elected to the Navajo Tribal Council, the governing body for the Navajo nation, was Annie D. Wauneka, who attended Fort Defiance Indian School for eleven years. One of her legislative colleagues was Irene Stewart, who started life with the name Goes to War With. The two women worked to improve health care and sanitation. Because of their efforts, tuberculosis ceased to be widespread among the Navajos.

Dr. Susan La Flesche, the Hampton graduate, also returned to her childhood home. Dr. La Flesche served her tribe in Nebraska as doctor, translator, and financial adviser, laboring for years to raise money to build the first community hospital on the Omaha Reservation.

One of the most dramatic journeys from traditional Native American life to political leadership was taken by Charles Eastman. The U.S. Cavalry had attacked his village when he was a boy named Ohiyesa. The women and children fled to Canada, while his father, Many Lightings, joined other Sioux warriors in a war against the whites. After several months of fighting, the cavalry captured Many Lightings. Ohiyesa was told that his father had been hanged. To avenge his father's execution, the boy vowed to kill all white people. But the report of the hanging proved false. Many Lightings had been pardoned by President Abraham Lincoln.

In the 1870s, at the urging of his father, Eastman walked from

Charles Eastman, an Indian school graduate who became a prominent doctor, author, and Indian rights advocate.
LIBRARY OF CONGRESS

his reservation in South Dakota to the Santee Normal Training School in Nebraska. In the classroom, the young man marveled that he "absorbed knowledge through every pore. The more I got, the larger my capacity grew, and my appetite increased in proportion." Eastman enrolled at Dartmouth College and then attended medical school at Boston University. The Sioux doctor became a popular writer and speaker. He wrote ten books about Indian life on the northern plains, and he told his stories to audiences in England and the United States.

Several other Indian school graduates became writers. Luther

Standing Bear, who spent five years at Carlisle, wrote popular books and magazine articles about the Sioux and worked as a Hollywood actor. Gertrude Simmons, who became Gertrude Bonnin after her marriage, published a series of influential magazine articles about her early tribal life and her years at white boarding schools.

Bonnin embraced her Sioux heritage by adopting an Indian name, Zitkala-Sa, or Red Bird. She and her husband taught at reservation schools in Utah and South Dakota before they moved to Washington, D.C., where Zitkala-Sa spent the rest of her life advocating women's and Indians' rights.

Both Zitkala-Sa and Eastman belonged to the Society of American Indians. This was the first political activist organization made up exclusively of Native Americans. The society's members represented many different tribes. United by their BIA school backgrounds, these men and women were concerned less with tribal differences than with the problems Indians faced living in a nation dominated by white people.

Eastman, Zitkala-Sa, and a number of other society members were nicknamed Red Progressives because of their political activism. The Red Progressives worked to improve life on all reservations, to promote understanding of Indian traditions, and to urge Congress to enact laws compensating Native Americans for the many broken treaties of the past. One of their biggest legislative victories was the Indian Citizenship Act of 1924, which made all Native Americans citizens. The country's first residents had finally become legal citizens of the United States.

Zitkala-Sa was an adult when she took a Sioux name and began dressing in the traditional style. BRIGHAM YOUNG UNIVERSITY PHOTOGRAPHIC ARCHIVES

Native Americans who had been armed with the white man's education, like Zitkala-Sa and Charles Eastman, were able to defend themselves against ignorance and prejudice while helping to preserve their unique heritage.

9

WHAT HAPPENED TO INDIAN SCHOOLS?

THE RED PROGRESSIVES were among the many critics of BIA education. Zitkala-Sa, in her widely read series of magazine articles, described the sad experience of being separated from her home and tribe. "Like a slender tree, I had been uprooted from my mother, nature, and God," she wrote. "I was shorn of my branches, which had waved in sympathy and love for home and friends."

BIA officials began to understand that a few years of school could not erase centuries of Indian traditions. Also, many white people were beginning to value Indian culture.

"I have none of the prejudice which exists in many minds against the perpetuation of Indian music and other arts, customs, and traditions," said Francis Leupp, the BIA commissioner. "It helps to make easier the perilous and difficult bridge which they are crossing at this stage of their development."

Years after Commissioner Leupp made this remark, the U.S.

Congress passed the Indian Reorganization Act of 1934, which officially introduced the teaching of Indian history and culture in BIA schools. The U.S. government had at last given up trying to make Indians think and live like white people.

Because of changing attitudes about Native American life, the government closed many off-reservation boarding schools and opened more day schools. Carlisle was one of the first Indian schools to be shut.

The Pennsylvania school had been the crown jewel of the Indian school system for the twenty-five years that Captain Pratt was superintendent. He forcifully defended his idea of completely removing Indians from their tribes and immersing them in white society. But many people disagreed with him, especially about taking children away from their parents. Carlisle's troubles began in 1904, when Captain Pratt was forced to resign as superintendent. The army officer's strong and inflexible opinions about Indian education had won him more enemies than friends.

After Pratt left, Carlisle had two weak superintendents. Under their administrations there were scandals involving drunken students, pregnant coeds, and pampered athletes. After an eighteen-year-old girl was held by two matrons while a male teacher beat her, some 250 students signed a petition asking Congress to investigate conditions at the school. The investigation found widespread abuse and mismanagement. Carlisle was closed in 1918, and the remaining students transferred to Haskell, Chilocco, Phoenix, and other schools out west.

By the end of the twentieth century, the number of off-

Alumni held reunions even after their schools no longer existed.

reservation boarding schools had declined to seven. Four of them date from the nineteenth century: Chemawa Indian School in Salem, Oregon; Riverside Indian School in Anadarko, Oklohoma; Sherman Indian High School in Riverside, California; and Flandreau Indian School in Flandreau, South Dakota.

These schools are still part of a large, far-flung BIA system. Some fifty thousand students attend more than two hundred schools either operated or funded by the BIA. They include the seven off-reservation boarding schools, twenty-five junior colleges, and numerous elementary and high schools. The majority of these schools are in the Southwest and in the upper Midwest, where the largest number of Native Americans live.

Unlike the earliest schools which were completely controlled by white people, most of today's Indian schools, are operated by tribes and their locally elected school boards. Students no longer wear military-style uniforms, march to the dining room, scrub classroom floors, or get locked in the guardhouse for misbehaving. They are not taught that the white man's way is the best or the only way. Indian history and traditions are important parts of their education, just as they are a valued part of America's history.

FOR FURTHER INFORMATION

Reading for Young People

Peter Anderson's *Charles Eastman: Physician, Reformer, Native American Leader* (Chicago: Children's Press, 1992). Charles Eastman's *Indian Boyhood* (New York: Time-Life Books, 1993) is a well-written, although somewhat romanticized, account of his Native American childhood. Jeri Ferris's *Native American Doctor: The Story of Susan LaFlesche Picotte* (Minneapolis: Carolrhoda Books, 1991) tells the story of the doctor's accomplished life. Jewel H. Grutman and Gaye Matthaie's *The Ledgerbook of Thomas Blue Eagle* (New York: Lickle Publishing Inc., 1997) is historical fiction. Nicely illustrated by Adam Cvijanovic, the book tells the story in pictographs and words of an Indian boy who is taken to Carlisle. Doreen Rappaport's *The Flight of Red Bird: The Life of Zitkala-Sa* (New York: Penguin, 1997) is a biography of Gertrude Simmons Bonnin. Ann Rinaldi's *My Heart Is on the Ground: The Diary of Nannie Little Rose, a Sioux Girl* (New York: Scholastic, 1999) is the fictional diary of a Sioux girl at Carlisle. Luther Standing Bear's *My Indian Boyhood* (Lincoln: University of Nebraska Press, 1988) is about his childhood before Carlisle. Gloria Whelan's *The Indian School* (New York: HarperCollins, 1996) is a novel about a girl who moves to northern Michigan to live with her aunt and uncle, who run a missionary school for Indian children.

Web Sites

http://www.epix.net/~landis is a Web page devoted to the Carlisle Indian School. Developed by Cumberland Valley Historical Society researcher

Barbara Landis, this site includes a brief history of Carlisle, short biographies of students, photographs, and links to related sites.

http://anpaserver.ualr.edu is the Web site for the American Native Press Archives, "one of the world's largest repositories" of Native American newspapers, magazines, and other printed materials.

http://hanksville.phast.umass.edu/misc/NAresources.html is the Index of Native American Resources on the Internet.

BIBLIOGRAPHY

Adams, David Wallace. *Education for Extinction: American Indians and the Boarding School Experience, 1875–1928.* Lawrence: University Press of Kansas, 1995.

Andrist, Ralph K. *The Long Death: The Last Days of the Plains Indians.* New York: Macmillan, 1964.

Betzinez, Jason. *I Fought with Geronimo.* Lincoln: University of Nebraska Press, 1959.

Brown, Dee. *Bury My Heart at Wounded Knee: An Indian History of the American West.* New York: Holt, Rinehart, and Winston, 1970.

Coleman, Michael C. *American Indian Children at School, 1850–1930.* Jackson: University Press of Mississippi, 1993.

Debo, Angie. *A History of the Indians of the United States.* Norman: University of Oklahoma Press, 1970.

Eastman, Charles. *From Deep Woods to Civilization.* Lincoln: University of Nebraska Press, 1977.

————. *Indian Boyhood.* New York: Time-Life Books, 1993.

Jackson, Curtis E., and Marcia J. Galli. *A History of the Bureau of Indian Affairs and Its Activities Among Indians.* San Francisco: R&E Research Associates, 1977.

Kabotie, Fred. *Hopi Indian Artist.* Flagstaff: Museum of Northern Arizona and Northland Press, 1977.

Lowawaima, K. Tsianina. *They Called It Prairie Light: The Story of Chilocco Indian School.* Lincoln: University of Nebraska Press, 1994.

Pratt, Richard Henry. *Battlefield and Classroom: Four Decades with the American Indian, 1867–1904.* Lincoln: University of Nebraska Press, 1981.

Standing Bear, Luther. *Land of the Spotted Eagle.* Lincoln: University of Nebraska Press, 1978.

———. *My Indian Boyhood.* Lincoln: University of Nebraska Press, 1988.

———. *My People the Sioux.* Lincoln: University of Nebraska Press, 1975.

Stewart, Irene. *A Voice in Her Tribe: A Navajo Woman's Own Story.* Socorro, N.M.: Ballena Press, 1980.

Talayesva, Don. *Sun Chief: The Autiobiography of a Hopi Indian.* Edited by Leo W. Simmons. New Haven: Yale University Press, 1942.

Trennert, Robert A., Jr. *The Phoenix Indian School: Forced Assimilation in Arizona, 1891–1935.* Norman: University of Oklahoma Press, 1988.

Utley, Robert M. *The Indian Frontier of the American West, 1846–1890.* Alburquerque: University of New Mexico Press, 1984.

Whitewolf, Jim. *The Autobiography of a Kiowa Apache Indian.* Edited by Charles S. Brant. New York: Dover, 1969.

Wilson, Raymond. *Ohiyesa: Charles Eastman, Santee Sioux.* Chicago: University of Illinois Press, 1983.

Yava, Albert. *Big Falling Snow: A Tewa-Hopi Indian's Life and Times and the History and Traditions of His People.* Edited by Harold Courlander. Albuquerque: University of New Mexico Press, 1978.

INDEX

Page numbers in **boldface** refer to illustrations.

About the Author

MICHAEL L. COOPER is a professional writer whose articles have appeared in publications such as *The Washington Post* and *Travel & Leisure*. He is the author of seven previous books for young readers, including, most recently, *The Double V Campaign: African Americans and World War II* (Lodestar Books). Mr. Cooper lives in Washington, D.C.